ATVs

BY JACK DAVID

BELLWETHER MEDIA • MINNEAPOLIS, MN

Are you ready to take it to the extreme?
Torque books thrust you into the action-packed world of sports, vehicles, and adventure. These books may include dirt, smoke, fire, and dangerous stunts.

WARNING: READ AT YOUR OWN RISK!

This edition first published in 2008 by Bellwether Media.

No part of this publication may be reproduced in whole or in part without written permission of the publisher. For information regarding permission, write to Bellwether Media Inc., Attention: Permissions Department, Post Office Box 19349, Minneapolis, MN 55419.

Library of Congress Cataloging-in-Publication Data

David, Jack, 1968–
  ATVs / by Jack David.
      p. cm. -- (Torque—cool rides)
  Summary: "Amazing photography accompanies engaging information about ATVs. The combination of high-interest subject matter and light text is intended for students in grades 3 through 7"--Provided by publisher.
  Includes bibliographical references and index.
  ISBN-13: 978-1-60014-146-1 (hardcover : alk. paper)
  ISBN-10: 1-60014-146-3 (hardcover : alk. paper)
  1. All terrain vehicles--Juvenile literature. I. Title.
TL235.6.D38 2008
  629.22'042--dc22

                                                                    2007040560

Contents

What Is an ATV?

An ATV is an all-**terrain** vehicle. ATVs are small, fast, and able to handle just about any type of terrain. ATVs are built for off-road riding. They are designed to ride on dirt, sand, mud, grass, or anywhere else a rider can take them.

Most models have four wheels. They're called "four-wheelers." Other models have three or even six wheels. All ATVs are designed to take riders where they can't go on ordinary vehicles.

Fast FaCt

Four-wheelers are also called "quads" or "quad bikes." Three-wheelers are also called "trikes."

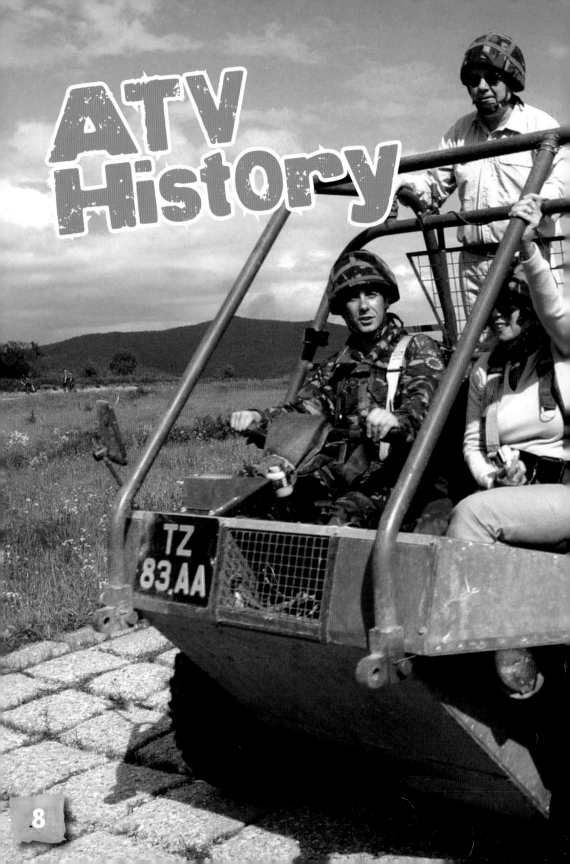

ATV History

ATVs have been around since the 1960s. The earliest models had six or eight wheels. They had small engines and moved slowly. They could handle any type of terrain.

People wanted something faster. Three-wheelers came out in the 1970s. Their lightweight build made them much faster than earlier ATVs. Four-wheelers became popular in the 1980s. They were lightweight and their small engines had even more power than earlier models. They were faster and more stable than three-wheelers.

Fast FaCt

Honda introduced the first three-wheeler to the United States in 1970.

Parts of an ATV

Good **traction** is the most important feature of an ATV. **Four-wheel drive** allows the engine to power all four wheels. This means that in order for an ATV to be able to move, only one of its wheels needs to have traction. Each wheel has its own **suspension system** of springs and shock absorbers. The special tires have deep **tread.** The bumps and grooves of the tread allow each tire to grip slippery terrain.

Fast FaCt

Sport model ATVs have stronger suspension systems and larger, more powerful engines than standard ATVs.

14

An ATV engine is small. It sits below the rider's seat. Engines are measured in cubic centimeters (cc). The area measured is space inside the **cylinder** where fuel is burned. Few ATVs have an engine larger than 500cc. Small engines produce plenty of power to keep lightweight ATVs moving fast. A powerful ATV can reach speeds of more than 70 miles (112 kilometers) per hour.

A rider controls an ATV with a pair of handlebars. The **throttle** is on the right handlebar. It controls the ATV's speed. The brake is on the left. It slows down and stops the ATV. ATVs also have a separate **stop switch**. Riders wear a cord around their wrist. The cord is attached to the stop switch. The ATV's engine shuts off if the rider falls.

ATVs in Action

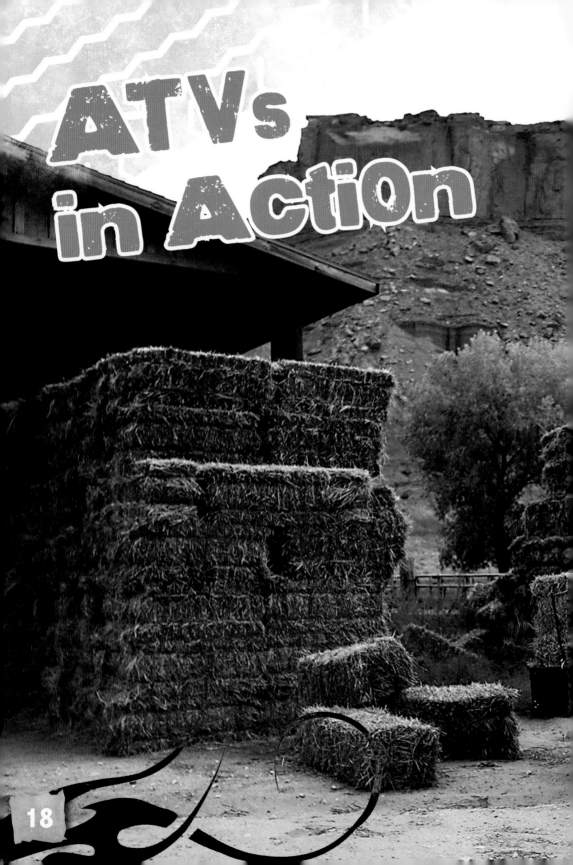

ATVs are great for both work and play. Farmers use ATVs to move around their fields. Ranchers use them to herd cattle. Rescue teams drive them to difficult-to-reach locations. And all kinds of people ride them just for fun.

Some people even race ATVs. **ATV motocross** is a growing sport. Riders race on dirt courses. They go around sharp turns and sail over big jumps. ATV motocross is an exciting sport that shows off the power of these small vehicles.

Fast Fact

ATV motocross races can take place in the woods, in the desert, on race-tracks, and even on ice.

Glossary

ATV motocross—a sport in which riders race ATVs on dirt courses with many jumps and sharp turns

cylinder—a part of an engine where fuel is burned; most engines have several cylinders.

four-wheel drive—a system in which the engine provides power to all four of a vehicle's wheels

stop switch—a switch on an ATV that shuts off the engine

suspension system—the springs and shock absorbers that connect the body of an ATV to its wheels

terrain—the natural surface features of the land

throttle—a lever that controls the speed of an ATV

traction—the grip of the tires on a riding surface

tread—the series of bumps and grooves on a tire that help it grip rough surfaces

To Learn More

AT THE LIBRARY

Anderson, Jenna. *How It Happens at the ATV Plant*.
Minneapolis, Minn.: Clara House, 2004.

Maurer, Tracy. *ATV Riding*. Vero Beach, Fla.:
Rourke, 2003.

Savage, Jeff. *ATVs*. Mankato, Minn.: Capstone, 2004.

ON THE WEB

Learning more about ATVs
is as easy as 1, 2, 3.

1. Go to www.factsurfer.com

2. Enter "ATVs" into search box.

3. Click the "Surf" button and you will
   see a list of related web sites.

With factsurfer.com, finding more information is
just a click away.

Index